BY ANJA BELLE

Knitting Double

Mastering the Two-Color Technique with Over 30 Reversible Projects

TRAFALGAR SQUARE
North Pomfret, Vermont

First published in the United States of America
in 2014 by
Trafalgar Square Books
North Pomfret, Vermont 05053

Originally published in German as *Doubleface stricken*.

ISBN: 978-1-57076-604-6

Library of Congress Control Number: 2013937968

Translation by Donna Druchunas
Diagrams: Anja Belle
Photography: frechverlag GmbH; Michael Ruder
Graphic design: Karoline Steidinger

Printed in China

10 9 8 7 6 5 4 3 2

▶28

▶16

▶66

CONTENTS

Knitting in the Next Dimension

Not long ago, the term "double knitting" meant no more to me than a small paragraph in a knitting book—not worth mentioning and certainly not suitable to knit anything meaningful with. The book you hold in your hands proves that there is much more to it!

Double knitting—that's knitting in the next dimension. Because, as you look at the stitches and turn your work, there is no back, no laborious weaving in or twisting colors, no rolling edges, and no ugly wrong side. Only two right sides with refined patterns! In short, double knitting is not wishful thinking; it actually creates the perfect piece of knitting.

Once you are familiar with the technique, there will be no stopping you. There is nothing that cannot be double knit: stunning accessories such as thick winter socks and color patterned scarves with two right sides, as well as practical items such as pot holders and oven mitts to protect your hands from heat in the kitchen.

But be warned: double knitting can become an addiction. It's just too exciting to see how an image or a pattern is created on the needles row by row. Once you get started, you can't stop. You have to knit "just one more row" to see a little more of the pattern …

Dive with me into a completely different type of knitting!

Anja Belle

Accessories

Accessories made with double knitting are true quick-change artists: agile, flexible, and versatile. With two right sides, the same scarf, hat, or mittens can change into completely different accessories, depending on which side is worn facing out. In practical terms, the double layer will protect you from the cold and wind. Even with a double layer, the accessories you knit with thinner yarns will still be delicate and elegant.

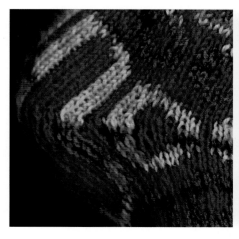 

Polka Dot Reversible Scarf
switch it up

SKILL LEVEL
Intermediate

SIZE
One size

FINISHED MEASUREMENTS
Approx. 82¾ x 5¼ in / 210 x 13.5 cm

YARN
CYCA #2, Schachenmayr Original Micro or equivalent (158 yd/144 m / 50 g; 100% microfiber)

YARN AMOUNTS
White 01, 50 g

Purple 48, 150 g

NEEDLES
U.S. sizes 2-3 / 3 mm: 60 in / 150 cm circular

NOTIONS
4 stitch markers

GAUGE
24 sts and 33 rows in double knitting = 4 x 4 in / 10 x 10 cm.

Adjust needle size to obtain correct gauge if necessary.

PATTERN STITCH
Double knitting worked back and forth in rows

Instructions

With a single strand of Purple, CO 634 sts (see page 74).
Setup row: *With White k1, with Purple p1 (1 st pair made); rep from * across—317 stitch pairs.
Divide the sts into 5 segments, placing a marker after every 63 stitch pairs.
Work in double knitting following the chart: work selvedge st, beg each section with the st before the repeat, work the repeat section 3 times, and end with the st after the repeat, work selvedge st. Work a one-color selvedge (see page 75). Work chart Rows 1-44 once, increasing 2 sts per segment every other row as shown.
BO in Purple (see page 79).

Finishing

Weave in ends.

My Tips for You

Changing length The pattern is worked over a multiple of 12+1. To lengthen or shorten the scarf, simply add or remove multiples of 12 from each segment.

Casting on Cast on with 1 strand from each ball to avoid having to measure yarn for the long-tail cast-on.

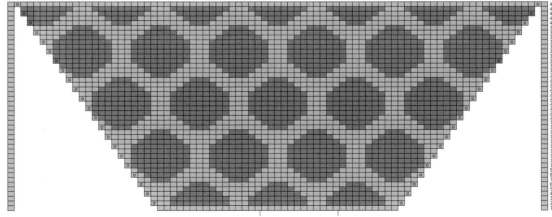

○ = Make 1 new stitch pair with yarnover inc (see page 76)

Repeat = 12 sts

Polka Dot Hat
knitted sideways

SKILL LEVEL
Intermediate

SIZE
One size

FINISHED MEASUREMENTS
Head circumference approx. 19½-21½ in / 50-55 cm

Length approx. 11¾ in / 30 cm

YARN
CYCA #2, Schachenmayr Original Micro or equivalent (158 yd/144 m / 50 g; 100% microfiber)

YARN AMOUNTS
White 01 and Purple 48, 100 g each

Small amount of smooth contrasting yarn the same size as cap yarn for provisional cast-on

NEEDLES
U.S. size 2-3 / 2.5-3 mm: 2 circulars

NOTIONS
Tapestry needle

GAUGE
24 sts and 33 rows in double knitting = 4 x 4 in / 10 x 10 cm.

Adjust needle size to obtain correct gauge if necessary.

PATTERN STITCH
Double knitting worked back and forth in rows

Instructions

With contrasting yarn, provisionally CO 122 sts.
Following the chart, create stitch pairs by working k1 with the front-layer color, p1 with the back-layer color across—61 stitch pairs.
The edge stitch on the straight side of the piece is worked as a selvedge stitch in one color (see page 75), and is not included on the chart.
Work short rows as charted, using the double knitting short-row turn (see page 78).
The stitches after the turning point remain unworked, and each row is 1 stitch shorter through chart Row 18. Beg with Row 19, each row is 1 stitch longer.
Work chart Rows 1-32 a total of 5 times.
Do not bind off.

Finishing

Remove the waste yarn from the provisional cast-on. Separate the 2 layers of fabric and place the live stitches onto separate needles.
Join beginning and ending rows with Kitchener stitch, working each layer of fabric separately.
Weave in ends.

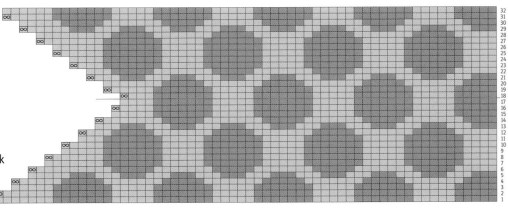

∞ = Turning Stitch pair (see page 78)

A Scrunchie

to keep your hair in place

SKILL LEVEL
Intermediate

SIZE
One size

FINISHED MEASUREMENTS
Circumference approx.
3½ in / 9 cm

YARN
CYCA #2, Schachenmayr Original
Catania or equivalent (137 yd/
125 m / 50 g; 100% cotton)

YARN AMOUNTS
Peacock 146 and Pool 165,
approx. 10 g each

NEEDLES
U.S. size 0 / 2 mm: set of 5 dpn
and 2 extra needles

NOTIONS
Hair tie, approx. 1½ in / 4 cm
around

GAUGE
22 sts and 34 rnds in double
knitting = 4 x 4 in / 10 x 10 cm.
Adjust needle size to obtain
correct gauge if necessary.

PATTERN STITCH
Double knitting worked in
the round

Plaid Pattern

Rnds 1-3: (work 2 stitch pairs in Pool, 2 stitch pairs in Peacock) around.

Instructions

With the 2-color cast-on, CO 60 stitch pairs. Divide sts evenly on 4 dpn and join to work in the round, being careful not to twist sts.

Work 6 rnds in plain double knitting.

*On one ndl, separate the two layers of fabric, and insert the hair tie between the layers. Put the stitch pairs back on the needle, re-joining the two layers. Rep from * on all 4 ndls, making sure the hair tie is not twisted and the working yarn does not get trapped.

Work 3 rnds in plaid pattern, then BO in double knitting (see page 79).

Finishing

Weave in ends.

Hot to Trot

with a short-row heel and toe

SKILL LEVEL
Experienced

SIZE
Adult S (M, L)

Numbers given are for smallest size; larger sizes are listed within parentheses. If there is only one number, it applies to all sizes

FINISHED MEASUREMENTS
Circumference approx.
8 (8½, 9½) in / 20 (21.5, 24) cm
Foot length approx. 9¾ (10½, 10¾) in / 25 (26.5, 27.5) cm

YARN
CYCA #1, Schachenmayr Regia 4-ply and Regia 4-ply Color or equivalent (230 yd/210 m / 50 g; 75% wool, 25% nylon)

YARN AMOUNTS
Crazy Ocean 5447, 100 g
Bright Red 2054, 100 g

NEEDLES
U.S. size 0 / 2 mm: set of 5 dpn

GAUGE
30 sts and 48 rnds in double knitting = 4 x 4 in / 10 x 10 cm.
Adjust needle size to obtain correct gauge if necessary.

PATTERN STITCH
Double knitting worked in the round

Instructions

With the 2-color cast-on, CO 60 (64, 72) stitch pairs. Divide sts evenly on 4 dpn and join to work in the round, being careful not to twist sts.

Leg

Begin working in double knitting, following chart for your size—the repeat is worked 6 (8, 9) times around. After completing each motif, move the beg of the rnd 5 (4, 4) stitch pairs to the left as shown on the chart. Work in even in pattern until leg measures approx. 6¼ (6¾, 7) in / 16 (17, 18) cm long, ending with Rnd 6 (4, 4) of chart.

Heel

Work the heel back-and-forth on half of the stitch pairs (working each knit and purl pair in the colors in which they appear) as follows:
Work 30 (32, 36) stitch pairs, turn, work the next stitch pair as turning stitches (see page 78).
Work 29 (31, 35) stitch pairs, turn, work turning stitches.
Work 28 (30, 34) stitch pairs, turn, work turning stitches.
Continue in this fashion, working 1 less stitch pair on every row, until 10 (10, 12) stitch pairs are worked.
Work 2 rounds of all stitch pairs, working both legs of each turning stitch as a single stitch, working the leg in pattern as est.
Work the second half of the heel as follows:
Work 21 (23, 25) stitch pairs, turn, work turning stitch.
Work 11 (13, 13) stitch pairs, turn, work turning stitch.
Work 12 (14 , 14) stitch pairs, turn, work turning stitch.
Work 13 (15, 15) stitch pairs, turn, work turning stitch.
Continue in this fashion until all stitch pairs are worked.

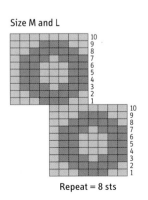

Size M and L

Repeat = 8 sts

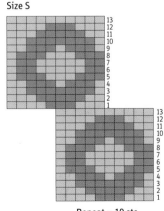

Size S

Repeat = 10 sts

Foot

Return to knitting in the round on all stitch pairs, following charted pattern. Work in pattern until foot measures 7 (8, 8¾) in / 18 (20, 22.5) cm.

Toe

Set aside the 30 (32, 36) sts on the top of the foot. Work the toe as for the heel on the 30 (32, 36) sts of the sole. Do not BO.

Finishing

Separate the layers of stitches on the toe and on the stitches set aside for the top of the foot. Join each layer with Kitchener stitch using matching colors. Weave in ends.

Make the second sock the same way.

Well Crossed Scarf
in half the knitting

SKILL LEVEL
Easy

SIZE
One size

FINISHED MEASUREMENTS
6¼ x 67 in / 16 x 170 cm

YARN
CYCA #1, Schachenmayr Regia Extra Twist Merino or equivalent (230 yd/210 m / 50 g; 75% merino, 25% nylon)

YARN AMOUNTS
Medium Grey 9358 and Charcoal 9359, 150 g each

NEEDLES
U.S. size 1-2 / 2.5 mm: circular

GAUGE
29 sts and 39 rows in double knitting = 4 x 4 in / 10 x 10 cm.

Adjust needle size to obtain correct gauge if necessary.

PATTERN STITCH
Double knitting worked back and forth in rows

Instructions

With Charcoal, CO 47 sts. In the first rnd, create stitch pairs as follows:
*With Charcoal, k1 and leave the stitch on the left needle, with Medium Grey, knit into the back of the same st, then drop the old stitch from the left needle; rep from * to end— 47 stitch pairs.

The selvedge stitches are worked in the color to match the pattern (see page 75) and are included in the chart.

Using double knitting, work Rows 1-24 of chart once, then repeat Rows 9-24 until scarf measures approx. 63 in / 160 cm. End by working rows 25-29 once.

Work 1 row plain with Charcoal as the main color, then BO in Charcoal (see page 79).

Finishing

Weave in ends.

My Tip for You

Twice as nice? Make two scarves to match different outfits!

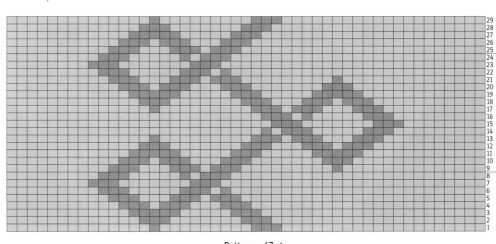

Pattern = 47 sts

Hand Warmers

an elegant accessory for that special occasion

SKILL LEVEL
Experienced

SIZES
S (M, L)

Numbers given are for smallest size; larger sizes are listed within parentheses. If there is only one number, it applies to all sizes

YARN
CYCA #2, Schachenmayr Original Micro or equivalent (158 yd/144 m / 50 g; 100% microfiber)

YARN AMOUNTS
Medium Grey 92 and Black 99, 50 (50, 100) g each

NEEDLES
U.S. size 1-2 / 2.5 mm

NOTIONS
Scrap yarn for putting stitches on hold

GAUGE
22 sts and 35 rnds in pattern = 4 x 4 in / 10 x 10 cm.

Adjust needle size to obtain correct gauge if necessary.

Eyelet Pattern

Rnd 1: *With Black, k2tog, yo; with Medium Grey, p2, backward yo (bring yarn over top of needle from back to front, then bring yarn between needles from front to back); with Black, sl 1, k1, psso; with Medium Grey, p2, (with Black, k1; with Medium Grey p1) 6 times; rep from * to the end of the needle.

Rnd 2: *(With Black, k2; with Medium Grey, p2) twice, (with Black, k1; with Medium Grey, p1) 6 times; rep from * to the end of the needle.

Instructions

With Black, CO 40 (44, 48) sts. Distribute sts evenly on 4 needles and join to work in the round, being careful not to twist sts.

In the first round, create stitch pairs as follows:

(With Medium Grey, k1 and leave the stitch on the left needle, with Black, knit into the back of the same st, then drop the old stitch from the left needle) 4 times. Now reverse the order of the colors and (with Black, k1; with Medium Grey k1tbl) 6 (7, 8) times; rep from * around—40 (44, 48) stitch pairs.

In the next rnd, reverse the order of the first 4 stitch pairs on each ndl for the eyelet pattern as follows: first 2 front layer sts, then 2 back layer sts, next 2 front layer sts, then 2 back layer sts. Do not change the position of the remaining sts. Place marker for beg of rnd. Work first 4 stitch pairs on each ndl in eyelet patt and rem stitch pairs in plain double knitting in the colors in which

they appear until piece measures approx. 4¼ in / 11 cm.

Thumb Gusset

Continue in pattern as established and *at the same time*, in the first and second Black stripes, work lifted bar increases (see page 79) every 3rd rnd 7 (8, 9) times as follows:

Work in pattern to 2nd Black stripe, work 2 stitch pairs, inc, work in pattern to last 2 sts of the next Black stripe, inc, work in pattern to end of rnd—set aside the 16/18/18 stitch pairs for the thumb with eyelet pattern centered on these sts.

CO 2 stitch pairs over the gap and arrange the sts evenly on 4 dpns with 10 (11, 12) sts per needle, and return to working in the round.

Work even for 1¼ in / 3.5 cm in pattern as set, then BO in Black as follows:
*Slip the second stitch (purl) of the stitch pair over the first stitch (knit), and drop it from the left needle. Next, knit the knit stitch with the main color. Rep from *, then pass the second stitch on the right needle over the first.
Repeat until all stitches have been bound off.

Thumb

Place the held thumb sts on the ndls and CO 2 stitch pairs over the gap by the hand. Divide the sts evenly on 3 dpns and join to work in the round. Work in pattern as set until thumb measures ½ in / 1.5 cm. BO as for hand.

Make a second mitt as for the first.

Finishing

Weave in ends, using matching color yarn tails to close up the small hole at the base of the thumb, fixing each layer separately.

From the Far North

warm and cozy

SKILL LEVEL
Easy

SIZE
One size

FINISHED MEASUREMENTS
Approx. 8 x 63 in / 20 x 160 cm

YARN
CYCA #2, Schachenmayr Original Baby Wool or equivalent (93 yd/85 m / 25 g; 100% merino)

YARN AMOUNTS
Black 99 and White 01, 150 g each

NEEDLES
U.S. sizes 3-4 / 3-3.5 mm: 16 in / 40 cm circular

GAUGE
24 sts and 34 rows in double knitting = 4 x 4 in / 10 x 10 cm.

Adjust needle size to obtain correct gauge if necessary.

PATTERN STITCH
Double knitting worked back and forth in rows

Instructions

With Black, CO 98 sts.
Row 1: (k1 White, p1 Black) across—49 stitch pairs.
There are no selvedge stitches worked.
Following chart, work Rows 1-24 a total of 20 times.
BO with Black (see page 79).

Finishing

Weave in ends.

My Tip for You

Contrast For a completely different look, use Black and a bright color, or use two different contrasting colors. You're limited only by your imagination.

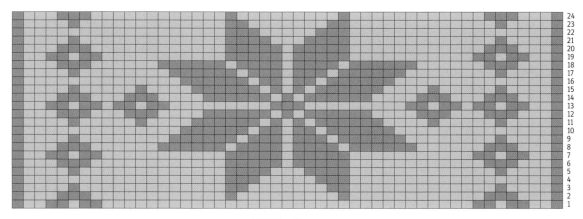

Pattern = 49 sts

Northern Star Hat

a traditional pattern

My Tip for You

Working the two layers of the
crown separately makes the work
go more quickly. Of course, you
may work the crown in double
knitting if you prefer.

Instructions

With the 2-color cast-on, CO 120 stitch pairs. Divide sts evenly on 4 dpn and
join to work in the round, being careful not to twist sts.
Follow chart working in double knitting, working the repeat 5 times around.

Crown

After 40 rnds have been worked (approx. 4 in / 10 cm), put the inner purl
stitches on hold and work on the outer layer with Black only as follows:
*Work in St st and, *at the same time*, k2tog 6 times, decreasing evenly spaced
around on every 3rd rnd 4 times. Next, decrease on every other rnd 5 times,
and then on every rnd 6 times. Now k2tog continuously until 6 sts rem. Break
yarn and run the tail through the remaining sts to gather together; fasten off.
Turn the hat to the other side and rep from * on the inner layer.

Finishing

Push the crown lining inside the hat so both layers are flush. Weave in ends.

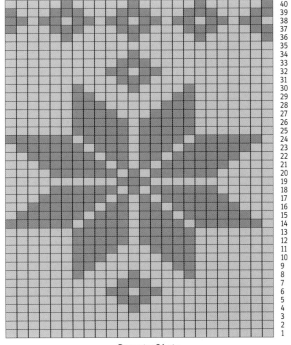

Repeat = 24 sts

Star Mittens

to match the scarf and hat

SKILL LEVEL
Experienced

SIZE
M (L)

Numbers given are for small size, with large size in parentheses. If there is only one number, it applies to both sizes

YARN
CYCA #2, Schachenmayr Original Baby Wool or equivalent (93 yd/85 m / 25 g; 100% merino)

YARN AMOUNTS
Black 99 and White 01, 75 (100) g each

NEEDLES
U.S. sizes 1-2 / 2.5 mm: set of 5 dpn

NOTIONS
Scrap yarn for putting stitches on hold

GAUGE
28 sts and 39 rnds in double knitting = 4 x 4 in / 10 x 10 cm.

Adjust needle size to obtain correct gauge if necessary.

PATTERN STITCH
Double knitting worked in the round

CHART
See insert in back of book.

Instructions

With Black, CO 52 (60) sts. Divide sts evenly on 4 dpn and join to work in the round, being careful not to twist sts.
*With Black, k1 and leave the stitch on the left needle, with White knit into the back of the same st, then drop the old stitch from the left needle; rep from * to end—52 (60) stitch pairs.

Cuff and Hand

Work in double knitting following the chart. For size L only, work the additional 8 stitch pairs as follows: with Black as MC and White as CC, 2 stitch pairs before column 1, after column 25, before column 28, and after column 52, and repeat chart Rows 26, 50, 74, and 93 each 3 times. *At the same time*, on Rnd 39 (42), begin thumb gusset shaping.

Thumb Gusset

Increase as charted, working increases using the lifted bar technique (see page 76). When all thumb gusset increases are complete there will be 18 (22) stitch pairs in the thumb. On Rnd 62 (66), put these sts on hold.

Hand

On the next rnd, CO 2 stitch pairs over the gap, and continue working pattern as charted.
On Rnd 85 (91), begin top shaping.

Top Shaping

Following chart, work decreases as follows: *on first ndl, work 1 stitch pair, decrease 2nd and 3rd stitch pairs together, work to last 3 sts on 2nd ndl, work next 2 stitch

pairs together as left-slanting decrease (see page 77-78), work last stitch pair on ndl; rep from * once more on ndls 3 and 4. Break yarn and, on each layer, run the tail through the remaining sts to gather together and fasten off.

Thumb

Put the 18 (22) held stitch pairs for the thumb onto 3 dpns and CO 2 stitch pairs over the gap. Work evenly in double knitting in colors as established until thumb measures 1¾ (2) in / 4 (4.5) cm.
Shape the thumb tip as follows:
Rnd 1: *Work 2 stitch pairs together as left-slanting decrease, work 1 stitch pair normally; rep from * around.
Rnd 2: Work all stitch pairs as they appear.
Rnd 3: (Work 2 stitch pairs together as left-slanting decreases) around.
Break yarn and, on each layer, run the tail through the remaining sts to gather together and fasten off.
Make the second mitten the same way.

Finishing

Close the small opening at the base of the thumb with small sewing stitches, working each layer separately with matching yarn.

My Tip for You

Fingerless gloves These mittens can also be made as fingerless gloves with one small change. Bind off after the third star on the hands, and after working about 1 in / 3 cm on the thumb.

Quick-Change Artist
smooth contrast

SKILL LEVEL
Experienced

SIZE
S (M, L, XL)

Numbers given are for smallest size, with larger sizes in parentheses. If there is only one number, it applies to all sizes

YARN
CYCA #1, Schachenmayr Regia 4-ply or equivalent (230 yd/210 m / 50 g; 75% wool, 25% nylon)

YARN AMOUNTS
Bright Red 2054 and Marine 324, 100 g each

NEEDLES
U.S. size 0 / 2 mm: set of 5 dpn

NOTIONS
Stitch holder or scrap yarn

GAUGE
30 sts and 48 rnds in double knitting = 4 x 4 in / 10 x 10 cm.

Adjust needle size to obtain correct gauge if necessary.

PATTERN STITCH
Double knitting worked in the round

CHART
See insert in back of book.

Instructions

With Marine, CO 56 (56, 64, 64) sts. Divide sts evenly on 4 ndls and join to work in the round, being careful not to twist sts. *With Marine, k1 and leave the stitch on the left needle; with Bright Red, knit into the back of the same st, then drop the old stitch from the left needle; rep from * to end—56 (56, 64, 64) stitch pairs. Place marker for beg of rnd.

Cuff and Hand

Work 3 (3, 4, 4) rnds in double knitting with Marine as MC, then work 2 (2, 3, 3) rnds with Bright Red as MC.
Begin working charted pattern over first 50 stitch pairs of rnd with Bright Red as MC and Marine as CC, and work rem stitch pairs in rnd with Bright Red as MC.

Thumb Gusset

On Rnd 21, pm after the 20th stitch pair and before the 23rd stitch pair, and inc using the lifted bar technique (see page 76). Rep inc inside markers every 4th rnd until there are 18 (20, 20, 22) stitch pairs in the thumb, working all new sts with Bright Red as MC. On the next rnd, put these sts on hold.

Palm

On the next rnd, CO 2 stitch pairs over the gap, and continue working pattern as set. On Rnd 70 (70, 74, 76), put the 44th-55th (44th-55th, 46th-59th, 46th-59th) stitch pairs on hold for the little finger. CO 2 stitch pairs over the gap and work 2 (2, 3, 4) more rnds.
Put all sts on hold.

Little Finger

Put the held 12 (12, 14, 14) st pairs back on ndls and CO 2 stitch pairs over the gap. Distribute evenly on 3 dpn. Work the CO sts with Marine as the MC, and work all other stitch pairs in the finger with Bright Red as the MC. Work even for 2 (2¼, 2¼, 2½) in / 5 (5.5, 6, 6.5) cm. Dec as follows:
Rnd 1: *Work right-slanting dec over first stitch pair, work 1 stitch pair normally; rep from * around.
Rnd 2: Work each stitch pair as it appears.
Rnd 3: (Work right-slanting dec over each two stitch pairs) around.
Break yarn leaving an 8 in / 20 cm tail, then, working on each layer separately, run the tail through the remaining sts to gather together and fasten off.

Ring Finger

CO 2 stitch pairs over new stitches at the inside of the little finger (the hole will be sewn closed when weaving in ends), place 7 (7, 8, 8) stitch pairs from the hand on the ndls, then CO 2 stitch pairs over the gap, then place 7 (7, 8, 8) stitch pairs from the other side of the hand on the ndls—18 (18, 20, 20) stitch pairs. Divide evenly on 3 dpns and join to work in the rnd. Work the 2 new stitch pairs on each side of the finger (4 total) with Marine as MC and work rem stitch pairs in finger with Bright Red as MC.
Dec when finger measures 2¼ (2½, 2½, 2¾) in / 6 (6.5, 7, 7.5) cm. Fasten off as for little finger.

Middle Finger

Work as for ring finger, and beg dec when finger measures 2¾ (3, 3, 3¼) in / 7 (7.5, 8, 8.5) cm. Fasten off as for little finger.

Index Finger

Place the rem 16 (16, 18, 18) stitch pairs on the ndls, CO 2 stitch pairs over the gap by the middle finger. Work the 2 new stitch pairs with Marine as MC and work rem stitch pairs in finger with Bright Red as MC and work Rnds 71-77 of chart.

Dec when finger measures 2 ¼ (2 ½, 2 ½, 2 ¾) in / 6 (6.5, 7, 7.5) cm. Fasten off as for little finger.

Thumb

Put the held stitch pairs for the thumb onto 4 dpns and CO 2 stitch pairs over the gap—22 stitch pairs. Work the 2 new stitch pairs with Marine as mc and work rem stitch pairs in finger with Bright Red as MC.

Dec when thumb measures 1¾ (2, 2, 2¼) in / 4 (4.5, 5, 5.5) cm.
Fasten off as for little finger.
Make the second glove the same, reversing the colors. When finished, turn inside out for a mirror image of the first glove. Or leave it right side out for opposite colors, as shown in the photo.

Finishing

Close the small openings at the base of the thumb and fingers with small sewing stitches, working each layer separately with matching yarn.

My Tips for You

Chart Mark the vertical line between the needles on the chart to help you keep track of your knitting.

Durability If you want to strengthen the single color parts of the glove, you can carefully twist the yarns around each other in 2-3 places on the thumb tip between the yarnover increases and the side of the fabric. When you do this, make sure that the following stitch is firmly worked so that the catches won't be visible on the right side.

Inca Style for the Feet
with a flap heel and band toe

Instructions

With Black, CO 64 sts. Divide sts evenly on 4 dpn and join to work in the round, being careful not to twist sts. The yarn tail marks the center back of the leg.
*With Monaco, k1 and leave the stitch on the left needle, with Black, knit into the back of the same st, then drop the old stitch from the left needle; rep from * to end—64 stitch pairs.

Leg

Work in double knitting and follow chart until leg measures approx. 4¼ in / 11 cm long. Mark your place on the chart so you can resume the pattern after working the heel.

Heel Flap

Working back and forth on the 32 sts on ndls 1 and 4, follow chart Rows 100-128. (Set sts on ndls 2 and 3 aside.) There are no selvedge sts.

Heel Turn

Work heel turn in plain double knitting with Black as the MC and Monaco as the CC as follows:
Next row (RS): Work 18 stitch pairs, work next 2 stitch pairs together as a left-slanting decrease (see page 77); turn.
Next row (WS): Slip the first stitch pair, making sure the working yarns are between the two layers; work 4 stitch pairs, work next 2 stitch pairs together as a right-slanting decrease (see page 78); turn.
Next row (RS): Slip the first stitch pair, work 5 stitch pairs, then work next 2

stitch pairs together as a left-slanting decrease; turn.
Continue in this fashion, working 1 more stitch pair before the decrease and turn, until all stitch pairs in the heel flap are worked.

Gusset Shaping

Return to working in the round and pick up and knit 15 sts on each side of the heel flap. Continue following the chart on all stitches, with the end of the round at the center of the bottom of the foot.
Decrease every other round as follows until 64 sts rem: Work the last 2 stitch pairs on ndl 1 as a right-slanting dec and the first 2 stitch pairs of ndl 4 as a left-slanting dec.

Foot

Work in pattern until foot is 6½ in / 16.5 cm long.

Toe

Continue following charted pattern and, *at the same time*, dec for toe as follows:
Dec rnd: Work to last 3 stitch pairs on sole, *right-slanting decrease, work next 4 stitch pairs as set, left slanting dec*, work to last 3 stitch pairs on instep; rep from * to * once, work as set to end of rnd.
Dec as above every 4th rnd 1 time, then every 3rd rnd twice, then every other rnd 4 times, then every rnd until 8 stitch pairs rem.
Cut both yarns, leaving an 8 in / 20 cm tail. Run each tail through the sts of the matching color and pull gently to gather in and fasten off toe.

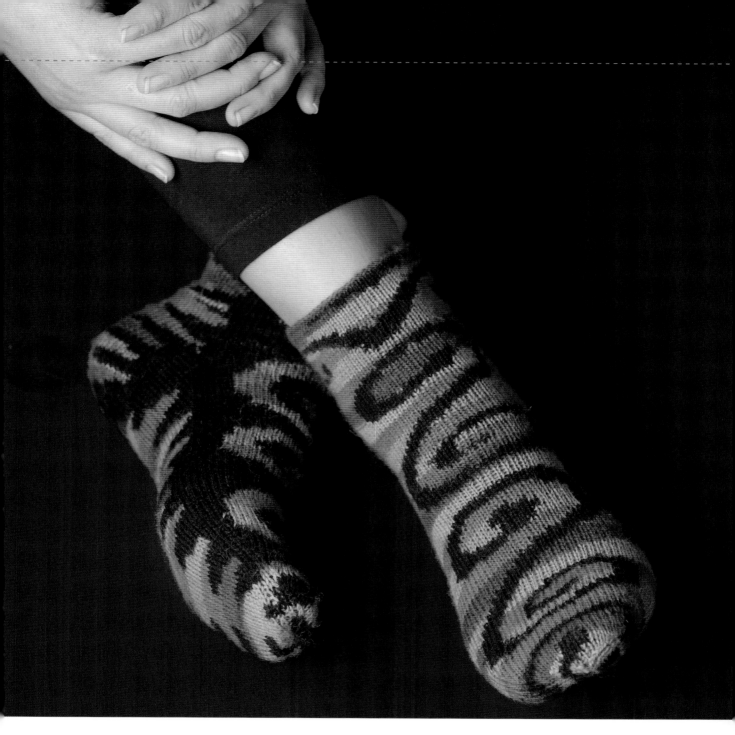

Finishing

Weave in ends.
Make the second sock the same way, reversing colors to create a mirror image of the design.

My Tips for You

Gusset Picking up the gusset stitches on each layer requires patience. It is easier if you use spare needles to separate the stitches of the front and back layers. Then you can place the stitches onto the working needle in the correct order.

Chart To help keep your place on the chart, mark a vertical line where you change needles.

Graceful Lily
the symbol of innocence and purity

SKILL LEVEL
Easy

FINISHED MEASUREMENTS
Approx. 6¼ x 63 in /
16 x 160 cm

YARN
CYCA #1, Schachenmayr
Regia 4-ply or equivalent
(230 yd/210 m / 50 g;
75% wool, 25% nylon)

YARN AMOUNTS
Purple 2020 and Black 2066,
150 g each

NEEDLES
U.S. size 1-2 / 2.5 mm:
circular

GAUGE
34 sts and 35 rows in
double knitting = 4 x 4 in /
10 x 10 cm.

Adjust needle size to obtain
correct gauge if necessary.

PATTERN STITCH
Double knitting worked back
and forth in rows

Instructions

With Black, CO 48 sts. In the 1st row, double the number of stitches as follows:
*With Purple, k1 and leave the stitch on the left needle, with Black, knit into the back of the same st, then drop the old stitch from the left needle; rep from * to end—48 stitch pairs.
Work the selvedge stitch in one color (see page 75).
*Work 10 rows in double knitting, working the colors as they appear. Then work charted pattern as follows: Work selvedge stitch, 2 stitch pairs in colors as they appear, work charted pattern across next 42 stitch pairs, work 2 stitch pairs in colors as they appear, work selvedge stitch.
Repeat from * 7 more times. Work 10 rows in double knitting, working the colors as they appear.
Binding off: *Slip the second stitch (purl) of the stitch pair over the first stitch (knit), and drop it from the left needle. Then knit the knit stitch with the main color. Rep from *, then pass the second stitch on the right needle over the first.
Repeat until 1 st rem. Cut the yarn and draw through last st to fasten off.

Finishing

Weave in ends.

Pattern = 42 sts

Flower Power Mittens

for a feeling of spring in winter

SKILL LEVEL
Intermediate

SIZE
Women's M

YARN
CYCA #1, Schachenmayr Regia 4-ply or equivalent (230 yd/210 m / 50 g; 75% wool, 25% nylon)

YARN AMOUNTS
Orange 1259 and Cardinal 1078, 100 g each

NEEDLES
U.S. size 0 / 2 mm: set of 5 dpn

GAUGE
34 sts and 47 rnds in double knitting = 4 x 4 in / 10 x 10 cm.

Adjust needle sizes to obtain correct gauge if necessary.

PATTERN STITCH
Double knitting worked in the round

CHART
See insert in back of book.

Instructions

With Cardinal, CO 56 sts. Divide sts evenly on 4 ndls and join to work in the round, being careful not to twist sts.
*With Cardinal, k1 and leave the stitch on the left needle, with Orange, knit into the back of the same st, then drop the old stitch from the left needle; rep from * to end—56 stitch pairs. Place marker for beg of rnd.

Cuff and Hand

Work in double knitting, following the chart.

Thumb Gusset

Increase as charted, working increases using the lifted bar technique (see page 76). When all thumb gusset increases are complete there will be 22 stitch pairs in the thumb. On Rnd 78, put these sts on hold.
On the next rnd, CO 2 stitch pairs over the gap, and continue working pattern as charted.
On Rnd 111, begin top shaping.

Top Shaping

Following chart, work decreases as follows:
*On first ndl, work 1 stitch pair, decrease 2nd and 3rd stitch pairs together, work to last 3 sts on 2nd ndl, work next 2 stitch pairs together as left-slanting decrease (see pages 77-78), work last stitch pair on ndl; rep from * once more on ndls 3 and 4.
Break yarn, leaving an 8 in / 20 cm tail; then, working on each layer separately, run the tail through the remaining sts to gather together and fasten off.

Thumb

Put the held stitch pairs for the thumb onto 4 dpns and CO 2 stitch pairs over the gap—22 stitch pairs. Work evenly in double knitting in colors as established until thumb measures 2 in / 4.5 cm.
Shape the thumb tip as follows:
Rnd 1: *Work 2 stitch pairs together as right-slanting decrease, work 1 stitch pair normally; rep from * around.
Rnd 2: Work all stitch pairs as they appear.
Rnd 3: (Work 2 stitch pairs together as right slanting decreases) around.
Fasten off as for the finger tips on the hand.
Make the second mitten the same way.

Finishing

Close the small opening at the base of the thumb with small sewing stitches, working each layer separately with matching yarn.

My Tip for You

Chart Mark the vertical line between the needles on the chart to help you keep track of your knitting.

Flower Power on Foot

with short-row heel and band toe

SKILL LEVEL
Experienced

SIZE
Women's L or Men's M

FINISHED MEASUREMENTS
Circumference approx.
8½ in / 21.5 cm

Foot length approx.
10½ in / 26.5 cm

YARN
CYCA #1, Schachenmayr
Regia 4-ply or equivalent
(230 yd/210 m / 50 g;
75% wool, 25% nylon)

YARN AMOUNTS
Orange 1259 and Cardinal
1078, 100 g each

NEEDLES
U.S. size 0 / 2 mm: set of
5 dpn

GAUGE
30 sts and 48 rows in double knitting = 4 x 4 in /
10 x 10 cm.

Adjust needle size to obtain
correct gauge if necessary.

PATTERN STITCH
Double knitting worked in
the round

CHART
See insert in back of book.

Instructions

With Cardinal, CO 64 sts. Divide sts evenly on 4 dpn (16 sts on each ndl) and join to work in the round, being careful not to twist sts.

Following the chart, *for each White square, with Cardinal k1 and leave the stitch on the left needle, with Orange knit into the back of the same st, then drop the old stitch from the left needle; and for each grey square, with Orange k1 and leave the stitch on the left needle, with Cardinal knit into the back of the same st; rep from * around—64 stitch pairs.

Place marker for beg of rnd.

Leg

Begin working in double knitting and follow chart.

Heel

Work the heel back and forth on half of the stitch pairs, working each knit and purl pair in the colors as charted (see page 78). The heel is worked as for the inca socks on page 28.

Foot

Return to knitting in the round on all stitch pairs following charted pattern.

Toe

Continue following charted pattern and, *at the same time*, dec for toe as follows:

Dec rnd: Work to last 3 stitch pairs on sole, *right-slanting decrease, work next 4 st-pairs as set, left slanting dec*, work to last 3 st-pairs on instep; rep from * to * once, work as set to end of rnd (see pages 77-78).

Dec as above every 4th rnd 1 time, every 3rd rnd twice, every other rnd 4 times, then every rnd until 8 stitch pairs rem.

Cut both yarns, leaving an 8 in / 20 cm tail. Run each tail through the sts of the matching color and pull gently to gather in and fasten off toe.

Make the second sock the same way, reversing the colors for a mirror image.

Finishing

Weave in ends.

Useful and Beautiful

Double knitting combines business with pleasure: Due to the double layer of fabric, these items are pretty to look at from all sides, and they are also very thick and provide insulation. The results are practical and decorative tools for everyday life.

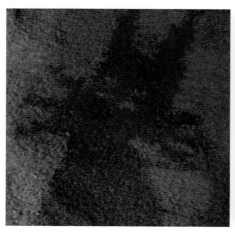 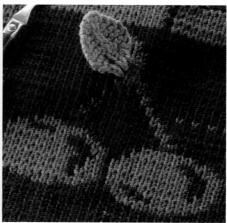

Bath Time

a splash of color

SKILL LEVEL
Easy

SIZE
L (S)

Numbers given are for large size, with smaller size in parentheses. If there is only one number, it applies to all sizes

FINISHED MEASUREMENTS
Length approx. 17¼ (13¾) in / 44 (35) cm
Width approx. 27½ (25½) in / 70 (65) cm

YARN
CYCA #3, Coats Puppets Lyric 8/8 or equivalent (76 yd/69 m / 50 g; 100% cotton)

YARN AMOUNTS
Light Teal 5057 and Dark Teal 5056, 200 (150) g each

NEEDLES
U.S. size 2-3 / 3 mm: circular

NOTIONS
Non-stick latex adhesive

GAUGE
20 sts and 29 rows in double knitting = 4 x 4 in / 10 x 10 cm.

Adjust needle size to obtain correct gauge if necessary.

PATTERN STITCH
Double knitting worked back and forth in rows

CHART
See insert in back of book.

Instructions

With the 2-color cast-on, CO 82 (64) stitch pairs. Work in double knitting following charted pattern. For the larger size, the pattern is 80 sts wide; for the smaller size, the pattern is 62 sts wide. For the smaller size, omit stitches 63-80, as indicated on the chart. Work a garter stitch selvedge with both colors (see page 75) on both edges. The selvedge stitches are not included on the chart.

After Row 198 (184), work last 2 rows of chart. Then BO all sts with both colors (see page 79).

Finishing

Weave in ends.

Trace the pattern lines on the back of the mat with the latex and allow to dry thoroughly overnight.

Felted Cat Bed

comfort for your kitty

SKILL LEVEL
Intermediate

FINISHED MEASUREMENTS
Diameter approx. 17¾ in /
45 cm

Height approx. 4¼ in / 11 cm

YARN
Shown: CYCA #6,
Schachenmayr Original
Wash + Filz it! (158 yd/
144 m / 50 g; 100% wool).

YARN AMOUNTS
Petrol 07 and Plum 26,
400 g each

SUBSTITUTION
Istex Léttlopi (109 yd/100 m
/ 50 g).

NEEDLES
U.S. size 10-11 / 6-8 mm:
circulars

GAUGE
12 sts and 18 rows in
double knitting = 4 x 4 in /
10 x 10 cm, before felting.

14 sts and 25 rows in
double knitting = 4 x 4 in /
10 x 10 cm, after felting.

Adjust needle size to obtain
correct gauge if necessary.

PATTERN STITCH
Double knitting worked
back and forth in rows

CHART
See insert in back of book.

Instructions

Bottom

With the 2-color cast-on, CO 30 stitch pairs. Work in double knitting, following charted pattern. Work slip-stitch selvedge with both colors (see page 75) on both edges. The selvedge stitches are included on the chart.

Work increases as charted using the lifted bar technique (see page 76). Work right-slanting decreases at the beginning of rows and left-slanting decreases at the end of rows (see pages 77-78).

On the last row, pass each purl stitch over its partnered knit, leaving the knits on the needle.

Sides

With MC, pick up 114 stitches around the edges of the piece so you have a total of 144 sts, including those already on the ndl. Join to work in the round.

*With MC, k1 and leave the stitch on the left needle, with CC, knit into the back of the same st, then drop the old stitch from the left needle; rep from * to end—144 stitch pairs. Place marker for beg of rnd.

Follow the chart for the fish motif, working the repeat 8 times around. BO with both colors (see page 79).

Finishing

Weave in ends. Felt the bed in the washing machine.

My Tip for You

Gauge Make a swatch first and felt your swatch because different yarns will felt differently.

To felt a knitted item, place it in a zippered pillow case and toss it in the washing machine. Set the machine for the smallest load size with hot wash, cold rinse, and a very small amount of soap. A few drops should do. Check the felting progress every five minutes. Some yarns will felt within the first few minutes, while others may need two or three cycles of agitation. You can keep moving the dial back to extend the agitation until the fibers begin to mat and the knitting stitches are no longer distinct.

When the item is felted and you don't want it to shrink any more, take it out and gently rinse it in tepid water in the sink.

Best Friends

a bed for your faithful companion

SKILL LEVEL
Intermediate

FINISHED MEASUREMENTS
Diameter approx. 17¾ in / 45 cm

Height approx. 4¼ in / 11 cm

YARN
Shown: CYCA #6, Schachenmayr Original Wash + Filz it! (158 yd/ 144 m / 50 g; 100% wool)

YARN AMOUNTS
Mango 04 and Dark Brown 22, 400 g each

SUBSTITUTION
Istex Léttlopi (109 yd/100 m / 50 g).

NEEDLES
U.S. size 10-11 / 6-8 mm: circular

GAUGE
12 sts and 18 rows in double knitting = 4 x 4 in / 10 x 10 cm, before felting.

14 sts and 25 rows in double knitting = 4 x 4 in / 10 x 10 cm, after felting.

Adjust needle size to obtain correct gauge if necessary.

PATTERN STITCH
Double knitting worked back and forth in rows

CHART
See insert in back of book.

Instructions

Bottom

With the 2-color cast-on, CO 30 stitch pairs. Work in double knitting following charted pattern. Work slip-stitch selvedge with both colors (see page 75) on both edges. The selvedge stitches are included on the chart.

Work increases as charted using the lifted bar technique (see page 76). Work right-slanting decreases at the beginning of rows and left-slanting decreases at the end of rows (see pages 77-78).

On the last row, pass each purl stitch over its partnered knit, leaving the knits on the needle.

Sides

With MC, pick up 117 stitches around the edges of the piece so you have a total of 147 sts, including those already on the ndl. Join to work in the round.

*With MC, k1 and leave the stitch on the left needle, with CC, knit into the back of the same st, then drop the old stitch from the left needle; rep from * to end—147 stitch pairs. Place marker for beg of rnd.

Follow the chart for the bone motif, working the repeat 7 times around. BO with both colors (see page 79).

Finishing

Weave in ends. Felt the bed in the washing machine.

My Tip for You

Felted projects are great for beginners because small mistakes and loose stitches will not show after felting.

To felt a knitted item, place it in a zippered pillow case and toss it in the washing machine. Set the machine for the smallest load size with hot wash, cold rinse, and a very small amount of soap. A few drops should do. Check the felting progress every five minutes. Some yarns will felt within the first few minutes, while others may need two or three cycles of agitation. You can keep moving the dial back to extend the agitation until the fibers begin to mat and the knitting stitches are no longer distinct.

When the item is felted and you don't want it to shrink any more, take it out and gently rinse it in tepid water in the sink.

A Casual Case

for your cell phone

SKILL LEVEL
Easy

FINISHED MEASUREMENTS
Approx. 3 x 4½ in /
8 x 11.5 cm

YARN
CYCA #2, Schachenmayr
Original Catania or equivalent (137 yd/125 m / 50 g;
100% cotton)

YARN AMOUNTS
Pool 165 and Royal 201,
50 g each

NEEDLES
U.S. size 0 / 2 mm:
straight and set of 5 dpn
for finishing

GAUGE
26 sts and 38 rows in
double knitting = 4 x 4 in /
10 x 10 cm.

Adjust needle size to obtain
correct gauge if necessary.

PATTERN STITCH
Double knitting worked
back and forth in rows

Stripe Pattern

*Work 5 rows with Pool as MC, 5 rows with Royal as MC; rep from * for patt.

Instructions

With the 2-color cast-on, CO 22 stitch pairs. Work in double knitting following stripe pattern for 4¼ in / 11 cm. Work garter selvedge with both colors (see page 75) on both edges. Divide layers and distribute 44 sts evenly on dpns (11 sts per ndl). BO in Pool.

Finishing

Weave in ends.

My Tip for You

Yarns Be sure to keep the working yarns between the two lay-ers of fabric as you work, so the knitting is worked as two lay-ers that can be separated to form the bag.

On a Roll

perfect for storing pencils—or better yet dpns!

SKILL LEVEL
Intermediate

FINISHED MEASUREMENTS
Approx. 8 x 9¾ in /
20 x 25 cm

YARN
CYCA #2, Schachenmayr Original Catania or equivalent (137 yd/125 m / 50 g; 100% cotton)

YARN AMOUNTS
Royal 201 and Red Wine 192, 50 g each

NEEDLES
U.S. size 0 / 2 mm: set of 5 dpn + 2 extra ndls

GAUGE
24 sts and 34 rows in double knitting = 4 x 4 in / 10 x 10 cm.

Adjust needle size to obtain correct gauge if necessary.

PATTERN STITCH
Double knitting worked back and forth in rows

Checkerboard Pattern

Worked over a multiple of 6 sts + 2 selvedge sts.

Row 1: *Work 6 stitch pairs with Royal as MC, 6 stitch pairs with Red Wine as MC; rep from * across.

Rows 2-9: Work all stitch pairs in the colors in which they appear.

Row 10: *Work 6 stitch pairs with Red Wine as MC, 6 stitch pairs with Royal as MC; rep from * across.

Rows 11-18: Work all stitch pairs in the colors in which they appear.

Instructions

With the 2-color cast-on, CO 50 stitch pairs. Work in double knitting following checkerboard pattern. Work slip stitch selvedge with both colors (see page 75).

Openings

When piece measures 3¾ in / 9 cm, create the openings as follows:
Separate the layers of each section, placing the stitches of the front and back layers on separate dpns. BO the sts on the front layer, leaving the last stitch on the ndl to work as k2tog with the first stitch on the next section. Double each stitch of the back layer as follows: with MC, k1 and leave the stitch on the left needle, with CC, knit into the back of the same st, then drop the old stitch from the left needle.

Work even on new stitch pairs until piece measures 9¾ in / 25 cm.

Finishing

Weave in ends.

For the ties, make two 4-stitch I-cords as follows: With Red Wine and dpn, CO 4 sts. *K4, do not turn, slide the sts to the other end of the dpn; rep from * until cord measures 32 in / 80 cm. BO.

Attach cords to case between the 4th and 5th rows of squares, with one cord attached at the side edge and the other between the 3rd and 4th columns of squares.

My Tip for You

Travel in style This case can easily be adapted as an on-the-road knitting toolkit. Use the pockets to hold crochet hooks for picking up dropped stitches, tape measures, and other small tools. Everything has its place. If you carry small items, fold the top of the roll down so they don't slip out of the pockets. You can easily change the number of pockets and width of each opening. Just be sure to work the color changes to match the width of the openings.

Sweet Dreams
cuddly baby blanket

SKILL LEVEL
Easy

FINISHED MEASUREMENTS
Approx. 32¼ x 32¼ in /
82 x 82 cm

YARN
CYCA #2, Schachenmayr
Original Baby Soft or
equivalent (77 yd/70 m /
50 g)

YARN AMOUNTS
Navy 150, 400 g
Vanilla 121, Mandarin 122,
Blue 153, and Rose 135,
100 g each

NEEDLES
U.S. size 2-3 / 3 mm:
circular and 2 dpn for
I-cord

GAUGE
21 sts and 29 rows in
double knitting = 4 x 4 in /
10 x 10 cm.
Adjust needle size to obtain
correct gauge if necessary.

PATTERN STITCH
Double knitting worked
back and forth in rows

CHART
See insert in back of book.

Instructions

Work 16 squares, each with the specified pattern and color (see chart below) as follows: With the 2-color cast-on, CO 48 stitch pairs. Work in double knitting following chart. Work slip stitch selvedge with both colors (see page 75). After all rows of chart are worked, BO with both colors (see page 79).

Finishing

Using Navy, sew squares together according to table. Work I-cord around edge of blanket using 2 dpn, Navy, and a CC as follows: CO 4. *K4, do not turn, slip sts to other end of dpn and draw working yarn snugly across back of work; rep from * until cord measures 129 in / 328 cm. Change CC every 8 in / 22.5 cm. Sew the cord around the outside edge of the blanket. Weave in ends.

My Tip for You

Motifs You can also make a blanket using the motifs from the potholder patterns on page 60 or 66. To make a larger or smaller blanket, simply make a different number of squares.

Heart Rose/Navy	Star Vanilla/Navy	Flower Mandarin /Navy	Butterfly Blue/Navy
Flower Mandarin/Navy	Butterfly Blue/Navy	Heart Rose/Navy	Star Vanilla/Navy
Star Vanilla/Navy	Flower Mandarin/Navy	Butterfly Blue/Navy	Heart Rose/Navy
Butterfly Blue/Navy	Heart Rose/Navy	Star Vanilla/Navy	Flower Mandarin /Navy

Striped Boxes
to hold little things

SKILL LEVEL
Easy

SIZE
S (L)

Numbers given are for small size, with large size in parentheses. If there is only one number, it applies to both sizes

FINISHED MEASUREMENTS
Approx. 2 x 2 x 2½ (2½ x 2½ x 2¾) in / 5 x 5 x 6 cm (6 x 6 x 7 cm)

YARN
CYCA #2, Schachenmayr Original Catania or equivalent (137 yd/125 m / 50 g; 100% cotton)

YARN AMOUNTS
Light Green 219 and Kiwi 212, 50 g each

NEEDLES
U.S. size 0 / 2 mm: set of 5 dpn

GAUGE
14 sts and 19 rows in double knitting = 2 x 2 in / 5 x 5 cm.

Adjust needle size to obtain correct gauge if necessary.

PATTERN STITCH
Double knitting worked back and forth in rows

Small Stripe Pattern
*Work 1 stitch pair with Light Green as MC, 1 stitch pair with Kiwi as MC; rep from * across.

Large Stripe Pattern
*Work 2 stitch pairs with Light Green as MC, 2 stitch pair, with Kiwi as MC; rep from * across.

Instructions

Bottom
With the 2-color cast-on, CO 16 (18) stitch pairs. Work in double knitting and small (large) stripe pattern for 19 (23) rows. Work slip stitch salvages with both colors (see page 75). BO with both colors (see page 79).

Sides
Make 4 pieces like the bottom, measuring 2¼ (2¾) in / 6 (7) cm tall.

Finishing
Sew pieces together with both colors. Weave in ends.

My Tip for You

Waterproof Spray the boxes with clear acrylic lacquer to make them waterproof so they are suitable for use in the kitchen or bathroom.

Hot Chilies

placemats with spice

SKILL LEVEL
Intermediate

FINISHED MEASUREMENTS
Approx. 18 x 10¼ in /
46 x 26 cm

YARN
Shown: CYCA #2,
Schachenmayr Original
Cotton Time (96 yd/88 m /
50 g; 100% cotton)

YARN AMOUNTS
Black 99 and Red 30,
150 g each
Small amount of Pesto 70

SUBSTITUTION
Schachenmayr Original Sun
City (106 yd/95 m / 50 g).

NEEDLES
U.S. size 1-2 / 2.5 mm:
circular and 2 dpn for
I-cord

GAUGE
22 sts and 34 rows in
double knitting = 4 x 4 in /
10 x 10 cm.
Adjust needle size to obtain
correct gauge if necessary.

PATTERN STITCH
Double knitting worked
back and forth in rows

CHART
See insert in back of book.

Instructions

With the 2-color cast-on using Black and Red, CO 105 stitch pairs (103 for the chart plus 2 selvedge stitches). Work in double knitting following the chart. Work slip stitch selvedge with both colors (see page 75); these stitches are not included on the chart. Work the stem in Pesto as follows: work both the knit and purl stitch in each stitch pair in Pesto, carrying both the Red and Black yarns between the two layers of fabric. At the beginning and end of the Pesto section, weave in the ends between layers.
BO with both colors (see page 79).

Finishing

Make a 1½ in / 3 cm I-cord for the stem: with Pesto and dpn, CO 3. *K3, do not turn, slip sts to other end of dpn and draw working yarn snugly across back of work; rep from * for desired length. BO. Attach the stem to the pepper on the right-side of the placemat.

Note: See the photo on page 55 which clearly shows the 3-dimensional chili stem.

Crunchy Cherries

add color to the table

SKILL LEVEL
Intermediate

FINISHED MEASUREMENTS
Approx. 18 x 10¼ in /
46 x 26 cm

YARN
Shown: CYCA #2,
Schachenmayr Original
Cotton Time (96 yd/88 m /
50 g; 100% cotton)

YARN AMOUNTS
Black 99 and Red 30,
150 g each
Small amount of Pesto 70

SUBSTITUTION
Schachenmayr Original Sun
City (106 yd/95 m / 50 g).

NEEDLES
U.S. size 1-2 / 2.5 mm:
circular and 2 dpn

GAUGE
22 sts and 34 rows in
double knitting = 4 x 4 in /
10 x 10 cm.

Adjust needle size to obtain
correct gauge if necessary.

PATTERN STITCH
Double knitting worked
back and forth in rows

CHART
See insert in back of book.

Instructions

With the 2-color cast-on using Black and Red, CO 105 stitch pairs (103 for the chart plus 2 selvedge stitches). Work in double knitting following the chart. Work slip stitch selvedge with both colors (see page 75); these stitches are not included on the chart.

Openings

Work the opening for the utensils on Row 66 as follows:
Work the selvedge st, then separate the layers of each section, placing the stitches of the marked stitch pairs on separate dpns. BO the sts on the front layer, leaving the last stitch on the ndl to work as k2tog with the first stitch on the next section. Double each stitch of the back layer as follows: With MC, k1 and leave the stitch on the left needle, with CC, knit into the back of the same st, then drop the old stitch from the left needle.
Continue working on the new stitch pairs until charted pattern is complete.
BO with both colors (see page 79).

Finishing

Work the cherry leaf in Pesto as follows: CO 5 sts and work 35 rows of I-cord (*k5, do not turn, slip sts to other end of dpn and draw working yarn snugly across back of work; rep from * for desired length). Do not BO.
Row 1: K2, yo, k1, yo, k2.
Row 2: K3, p1, k3.
Row 3: K3, yo, k1, yo, k3.
Row 4: K4, p1, k4.
Row 5: K4, yo, k1, yo, k4.
Row 6: K5, p1, k5.
Row 7: K4, k3tog, k4.
Row 8: K4, p1, k4.
Row 9: K3, k3tog, k3.
Row 10: K3, p1, k3.
Decrease the same way until 3 sts rem. Cut the yarn and draw the end through the rem 3 sts to fasten off. Sew the leaf on to the placemat using the chart as a guide.

Tangy Lemon Placemats

add zest to any table

FINISHED MEASUREMENTS
Approx. 19½ x 11¾ in / 50 x 30 cm

YARN
Shown: CYCA #2, Schachenmayr Original Cotton Time (96 yd/88 m / 50 g; 100% cotton)

YARN AMOUNTS
Black 99 and Sun 22, 100 g each
Small amount of Pesto 70

SUBSTITUTION
Schachenmayr Original Sun City (106 yd/95 m / 50 g).

NEEDLES
U.S. size 1-2 / 2.5 mm: circular

NOTIONS
Embroidery needle.

GAUGE
22 sts and 34 rows in double knitting = 4 x 4 in / 10 x 10 cm.

Adjust needle size to obtain correct gauge if necessary.

PATTERN STITCH
Double knitting worked back and forth in rows

CHART
See insert in back of book.

Instructions

With the 2-color cast-on using Black and Sun, CO 87 stitch pairs (85 for the chart plus 2 selvedge stitches). Work in double knitting following the chart. Work slip stitch selvedge with both colors (see page 75); these stitches are not included on the chart. BO with both colors (see page 79).

Finishing

Sew around edges of lemon seeds using Pesto. Weave in ends.

Splash of Color

double knitting, double color

Instructions

With the 2-color cast-on using Mandarin and Light Blue, CO 34 stitch pairs. Work in double knitting following the chart. Work slip stitch selvedge with both colors (see page 75); these stitches are not included on the chart.

Work 1 row of plain double knitting with Mandarin as the MC and Light Blue as the CC. Begin working charted pattern and changing colors as follows (first color is MC and second color is CC for each row):

Rows 1 and 2: Mandarin and Light Blue
Row 3: Mandarin and Medium Blue
Rows 4-6: Yellow and Medium Blue
Rows 7 and 8: Mandarin and Medium Blue
Rows 9 and 10: Mandarin and Light Blue

Repeat chart rows 1-10 4 times, then work 1 row without patterning as at the beginning. BO with both colors (see page 79). Do not cut yarn.

Finishing

Put the last loop on the crochet hook and crochet a chain approx. 2½ in / 6 cm long. Sew the end to the same corner to form a loop. Weave in ends.

My Tip for You

Fair Isle When you think of colorful knitting, the first thing that comes to mind is the wonderful multi-colored sweaters and cardigans in the traditional patterns from Fair Isle, Scotland. These sweaters are usually knit in the round, with the unused color stranded across the back of the work. Many traditional Fair Isle motifs are based on XOX, recurring crosses and circles, separated by subtle borders.

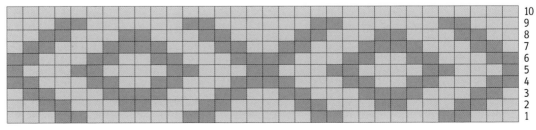

Pattern = 32 sts

Staycation

vacation in the kitchen

SKILL LEVEL
Easy

FINISHED MEASUREMENTS
Approx. 7 x 7½ in /
18 x 19 cm

YARN
Shown: CYCA #2,
Schachenmayr Original
Cotton Time (96 yd/88 m /
50 g; 100% cotton)

YARN AMOUNTS
Sun 22 and Pesto 70, 50 g
each

SUBSTITUTION
Schachenmayr Original Sun
City (106 yd/95 m / 50 g).

NEEDLES
U.S. size 1-2 / 2.5 mm:
circular

CROCHET HOOK
U.S. size B1-C2 / 2.5 mm

GAUGE
22 sts and 34 rows in
double knitting = 4 x 4 in /
10 x 10 cm.

Adjust needle size to obtain
correct gauge if necessary.

PATTERN STITCH
Double knitting worked
back and forth in rows

CHART
See insert in back of book.

Instructions

With the 2-color cast-on, CO 37 stitch pairs. Work one potholder following each of the double knitting charts. Work slip stitch selvedge with both colors (see page 75); these stitches are not included on the chart.
Do not cut yarn.

Finishing

Put the last loop on the crochet hook and crochet a chain approx. 2½ in / 6 cm long. Sew the end to the same corner to form a loop. Weave in ends.

My Tip for You

Matching potholders Of course you can make two potholders with the same motif. Change the MC and CC on the second potholder and you'll have a pair with mirror images.

Six-Sided Potholders

with romantic blossoms

SKILL LEVEL
Experienced

FINISHED MEASUREMENTS
Approx. 8 in / 18 cm circumference

YARN
Shown: CYCA #2, Schachenmayr Original Cotton Time (96 yd/88 m / 50 g; 100% cotton)

YARN AMOUNTS
White 01 and Pink 37, 50 g each

SUBSTITUTION
Schachenmayr Original Sun City (106 yd/95 m / 50 g).

NEEDLES
U.S. size 1-2 / 2.5 mm: circular and set of 5 dpn

CROCHET HOOK
U.S. size B1-C2 / 2.5 mm

GAUGE
22 sts and 34 rnds in double knitting = 4 x 4 in / 10 x 10 cm.

Adjust needle size to obtain correct gauge if necessary.

PATTERN STITCH
Double knitting worked in the round

Instructions

With the 2-color cast-on, CO 132 stitch pairs, leaving a tail approx. 19½ in / 50 cm long. Work potholder in double knitting, repeating the chart 6 times around. Dec 12 stitch pairs every other rnd as charted (see pages 77-78). When sts no long reach around circular ndl, change to dpn.

Finishing

After Rnd 22, cut the yarn and run each tail through the rem sts of the matching color layer, then gather together to fasten off. Using the beginning tails, crochet a chain and sew the end to the same corner to form a loop. Weave in ends.

◤ = right-slanting decrease (see page 78)
◣ = left-slanting decrease (see page 77)

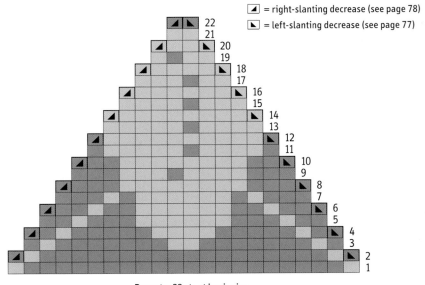

Repeat = 22 sts at beginning

Can Koozie

keep your drink cold

SKILL LEVEL
Easy

FINISHED MEASUREMENTS
Circumference approx.
8¼ in / 21 cm

Height approx. 8 in / 20 cm

YARN
CYCA #2, Schachenmayr
Original Catania or
equivalent (137 yd/125 m /
50 g; 100% cotton)

YARN AMOUNTS
Jade 253 and Navy 124,
50 g each

NEEDLES
U.S. size 0 / 2 mm: dpn

GAUGE
22 sts and 34 rnds in
double knitting = 4 x 4 in /
10 x 10 cm.

Adjust needle size to obtain
correct gauge if necessary.

PATTERN STITCH
Double knitting worked
back in the round

CHART
See insert in back of book.

Instructions

With Jade, CO 4 sts. Divide sts onto 2 ndls and join to work in the rnd.

Base

Begin working as a single layer as follows:
Rnd 1: Knit into the front and back of each st—8 sts.
Rnd 2: Knit into the front and back of each st—16 sts.
Rnd 3: (Kf/b, k1) around, divide sts onto 4 dpns.
Rnd 4: Knit.
Rnd 5: (Kf/b, k2) around, divide sts onto 4 dpns.
Rnd 6: Knit.
Rep last 2 rnds, working 1 more plain knit st after each kf/b inc until you have 56 sts.

Sides

Create stitch pairs for double knitting: *With Jade, k1 and leave the stitch on the left needle, with Navy knit into the back of the same st, then drop the old stitch from the left needle; rep from * around—56 stitch pairs.
Work in the round, working the charted pattern over the first 30 sts of the rnd and plain double knitting with Jade as the MC for the rest of the rnd.
When piece measures 8 in / 20 cm, BO as follows:
*Slip the second stitch (purl) of the stitch pair over the first stitch (knit), and drop it from the left needle. Then knit the knit stitch with the main color. Rep from *, then pass the second stitch on the right needle over the first.
Repeat until all stitches have been bound off.

Finishing

Weave in ends.

My Tip for You

Multi-purpose Need extra insulation for a cold soda or beer? Freeze the can cozy before pulling it over your can. Because it's made from 100% cotton yarn, it will be fine after the next washing. You can also use the dry cozy to keep hot drinks like coffee, tea, or mulled wine from scalding your hands.

Far-East Flair

with Chinese characters

SKILL LEVEL
Easy

FINISHED MEASUREMENTS
Approx. 6¾ x 6 in /
17.5 x 15.5 cm

YARN
Shown: CYCA #2,
Schachenmayr Original
Cotton Time (96 yd/88 m /
50 g; 100% cotton)

YARN AMOUNTS
Red 30 and Black 99,
50 g each

SUBSTITUTION
Schachenmayr Original Sun
City (106 yd/95 m / 50 g).

NEEDLES
U.S. size 1-2 / 2.5 mm:
circular

CROCHET HOOK
U.S. size B1-C2 / 2.5 mm

GAUGE
22 sts and 34 rows in
double knitting = 4 x 4 in /
10 x 10 cm.

Adjust needle size to obtain
correct gauge if necessary.

PATTERN STITCH
Double knitting worked
back and forth in rows

CHART
See insert in back of book.

Instructions

With Black, CO 37 sts.
Create stitch pairs for double knitting: *With Black, k1 and leave the stitch on the left needle, with Red, knit into the back of the same st, then drop the old stitch from the left needle; rep from * around—37 stitch pairs.
Work selvedge stitches in one color to form a contrasting border (see page 75); these stitches are not included on the chart. Work one potholder following each chart.
Bind off as follows: *slip the second stitch (purl) of the stitch pair over the first stitch (knit), and drop it from the left needle. Then knit the knit stitch with the main color. Rep from *, then pass the second stitch on the right needle over the first.
Repeat until all stitches have been bound off. Do not cut yarn.

Finishing

Put the last loop on the crochet hook and crochet a chain approx. 2 in / 4.5 cm long.
Sew the end to the same corner to form a loop. Weave in ends.

My Tip for You

Meaning The two characters mean "fire" and "eternity."

Not Just for the Wok
an oven mitt in red and Black

SKILL LEVEL
Intermediate

FINISHED MEASUREMENTS
Length: 9 in / 23 cm
Width: 10½ in / 27 cm

YARN
Shown: CYCA #2, Schachenmayr Original Cotton Time (96 yd/88 m / 50 g; 100% cotton)

YARN AMOUNTS
Red 30 and Black 99, 100 g each

SUBSTITUTION
Schachenmayr Original Sun City (106 yd/95 m / 50 g).

NEEDLES
U.S. size 1-2 / 2.5 mm: set of 5 dpn

GAUGE
22 sts and 34 rnds in double knitting = 4 x 4 in / 10 x 10 cm.

Adjust needle size to obtain correct gauge if necessary.

PATTERN STITCH
Double knitting worked in the round

Instructions

With the 2-color cast-on, CO 56 stitch pairs, leaving tail a little longer than usual. Divide sts evenly on 4 dpns (14 st pairs per ndl) and join to work in the round, being careful not to twist sts.

Work 5 rnds in double knitting with Black as MC and Red as CC.

Next rnd:

Ndls 1 and 2: Work 4 stitch pairs with Black as MC, 20 stitch pairs with Red as MC, 4 stitch pairs with Black as MC.

Ndls 3 and 4: Work 4 stitch pairs with Red as MC, 20 stitch pairs with Black as MC, 4 stitch pairs with Red as MC.

Work colors in this pattern until piece measures 2½ in / 6.5 cm long.

Thumb Gusset

Continue in pattern as established and, *at the same time*, inc as foll:

Before the last stitch pair on the second ndl and before the second stitch pair on the third ndl, work lifted bar increases (see page 76) every 3rd rnd until there are 12 stitch pairs increased. Work the increases on ndl 2 with Black as the MC and the increases on ndl 3 with Red as the MC. Set these stitches aside along with the stitch just before and just after the increase section—14 stitch pairs in thumb gusset.

Hand

On the next rnd, CO 2 stitch pairs over the gap, and divide sts evenly over 4 dpns. Continue working pattern as set. When piece measures 2 ½ in / 6.5 cm, begin top shaping.

Top Shaping

Next rnd: Work 28 stitch pairs with Black as MC, and the rest of the rnd with Red as MC.

Continue in patt as est and, *at the same time*, work decreases as follows: *on first ndl, work 1 stitch pair, decrease 2nd and 3rd stitch pairs together, work to last 3 sts on 2nd ndl, work next 2 stitch pairs together as left-slanting decrease (see page 77-78), work last stitch pair on ndl; rep from * once more on ndls 3 and 4.

Dec every other rnd 6 times, then every rnd until 8 stitch pairs rem.

Break yarn and, on each layer, run the tail through the remaining sts to gather together and fasten off.

Thumb

Put the 14 held stitch pairs for the thumb onto 3 dpns and CO 2 stitch pairs over the gap—16 stitch pairs.

Next rnd: Work 8 stitch pairs with Black as MC, 8 stitch pairs with Red as MC.

Work evenly in double knitting in colors as established until thumb measures 2 in / 5 cm.

Shape the thumb tip as follows:

Rnd 1: *Work 2 stitch pairs together as right-slanting decrease, work 1 stitch pair normally; rep from * around.

Rnd 2: Work all stitch pairs as they appear.

Rnd 3: (Work 2 stitch pairs together as right-slanting decreases) around.

Break yarn and, on each layer, run the tail through the remaining sts to gather together and fasten off.

Finishing

Weave in ends, using matching color yarn tails to close up the small hole at the base of the thumb in each layer separately. Use the tails to make a two-color twisted cord and sew the end of the cord to the inside of the mitt at the same place where the tails are attached. Make the second mitt the same way.

69

Christmas Decorations

ornaments for your tree

SKILL LEVEL
Easy

FINISHED MEASUREMENTS
Approx. 2 x 2 in / 5 x 5 cm

YARN
CYCA #2, Schachenmayr Original Catania Fine or equivalent (137 yd/125 m / 50 g; 100% cotton)

YARN AMOUNTS
Tomato 1002 and White 1000, 50 g each

NEEDLES
U.S. size 0 / 2 mm: set of 5 dpn

CROCHET HOOK
U.S. size B-1 / 2.25 mm

GAUGE
15 sts and 21 rows in double knitting = 2 x 2 in / 5 x 5 cm.

Adjust needle size to obtain correct gauge if necessary.

PATTERN STITCH
Double knitting worked back and forth in rows

Instructions

With the 2-color cast-on, CO 17 stitch pairs. Work one ornament following each double-knitting chart.
Work slip stitch selvedge with both colors (see page 75); these stitches are not included on the chart. BO with both colors (see page 79).
Do not cut yarn.

Finishing

Put the last loop on the crochet hook and crochet a chain approx. 2½ in / 6 cm long. Sew the end to the same corner to form a loop. Weave in ends.

My Tip for You

Structure The ornaments should be knit at a very tight gauge. If you want them to be stiffer, use spray starch.

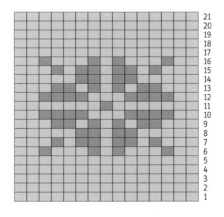

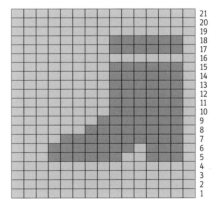

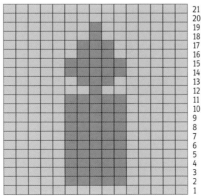

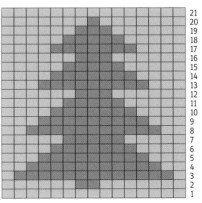

All patterns = 15 sts

Double-Knitting Techniques

Basic Double Knitting Technique

When you work double knitting, two layers of fabric are worked at the same time, each with a different color. The two layers are attached, and the resulting fabric has two right sides and no visible wrong side. The projects in this book can be turned over or inside out (if knitted in the round), and there are two "good" sides.

As you knit, both sets of stitches are on the same needle. You always knit one stitch for the front layer then purl the following stitch for the back layer.

Both working yarns must be carried between the two layers of fabric at all times: Hold both yarns in back when working a knit stitch and both in front when working a purl stitch. Each stitch is worked with only one color.

Each knit and purl form one stitch pair. The two parts of a stitch pair are each worked in a different color. So, if the first stitch is knit with the main color, the second stitch in the pair will be purled with the contrasting color. (The only exceptions in this book are the third color in the placemats on page 52 and the eyelets on the fingerless gloves on page 18.)

The pattern knitted in double knitting shows on both sides with the colors reversed like a mirror image. The background color is the main color, and the pattern color is the contrasting color. The main color becomes the pattern color on the back layer and the contrasting color becomes the background on the back layer.

When the knit stitch is worked in the main color, the following purl stitch is worked in the contrasting color.

When the knit stitch is worked in the contrasting color, the following purl stitch is worked in the main color.

With each color change, the yarns cross, and the two layers of fabric are firmly joined together.

Reading Double-Knitting Charts

All of the charts in this book have white and grey squares. The white square represents the main color, or the background. The dark grey always represents the pattern color. Once you knit a few rows, you will be comfortable with which color is used for each square and you won't have to keep checking the chart key.

Each square on the chart represents a stitch pair, that is, one knit and one purl stitch in different colors. When the chart square is white, the first stitch is knit with the main color and the second stitch is purled with the contrasting color. When the chart square is grey, the colors are reversed and the first stitch is knit with the contrasting color and the second stitch is purled with the main color.

Note: When working back and forth, on each row the main color and pattern color are reversed. When working in the round, the main color and pattern color remain the same and the work is not turned.

The charts are read following the direction of the knitting. Begin at the bottom right, and read the row across from right to left as you work a right-side row. After turning the knitted piece, follow the next chart row in reverse from left to right. When working in the round, all chart rows are read from right to left because you never turn your knitting around to go back in the other direction.

Casting On

Two-color Cast-on

In this technique, each stitch is cast on with two strands of yarn so you create stitch pairs immediately at the cast-on edge. On the first row, if the colors are out of sequence, switch the position of two stitches by passing one stitch over the other before working them. After the cast-on is complete, each stitch is worked separately as one part of a stitch pair, in the main color or contrasting color. Unless otherwise specified in the pattern, it does not matter which color is used as the main color.

One-color Cast-on

In this technique, for each stitch pair, one stitch is cast on with a single strand of yarn. On the first row or round, each stitch is doubled to form a stitch pair. First the stitch is knit through the front as usual with the main color, and the old stitch is left on the left needle. Then the same stitch is knit through the back with the contrasting color and the old stitch is dropped from the left needle. The side with the knit stitches is the right side of the work. On the back, purl bumps will show, indicating the wrong side.

Double-stranded Cast-on

Cast on normally with a double strand of yarn. Each double-stranded stitch will be worked as a stitch pair on the first round as follows: K1 with MC, p1 with CC (1 stitch pair created). In this technique, you cast on half the number of stitches needed for the first round. If the pattern doesn't specify, it does not matter which color you use for the cast on.

Holding the Yarn

Working with two colors at the same time will be unfamiliar at first and requires practice. There are several different ways to hold the yarn. All of the techniques will result in the same knitted fabric, so choose the method that is most comfortable for you.

Separating Strands with Your Middle Finger

Use your middle finger as a divider to separate the two strands of yarn. Hold the main color in front of your middle finger and the contrasting color behind it. In this way, the colors will not get twisted. Use your thumb and index finger to work the stitches.

When you change colors, the main color will now be behind your middle finger, and the contrasting color in front. With a little practice, catching the correct color will become automatic. Use your thumb to pull the desired color into place to work it. Rotate the strands first one way then the other so they don't get twisted or tangled.

Separating Strands with Your Index Finger

When you drape the yarn over your index finger, cross the two colors so the main color drapes over your finger from back to front and the contrasting color drapes over your finger from front to back.

Working with One Color in Each Hand

Carry the main color in your left hand and the contrasting color in your right hand.

Selvedge Stitches

Two-color Garter Stitch Selvedge

On each row, the first and last stitches are knit as one stitch with both strands of yarn held together.

Two-color Slip Stitch Selvedge

On each row, the first stitch pair is slipped together knitwise, and the last stitch pair is purled together with both colors as one stitch.

One-color Selvedge

On each row, the first and last stitch pairs are worked as double knitting in the opposite color of the background. If the stitch before the edge is the main color, work the edge stitch in the contrasting color, and vice versa.

Increasing

Lifted Bar Increases

Insert the right needle from front to back under the two bars between the stitch just worked and the next stitch.

Knit the front yarn through the back loop with the main color.

Purl the back yarn through the back loop with the contrasting color.

Yarnover Increase

Work in pattern to the place indicated in the chart to increase. Yarn over with both yarns together. Complete the row normally.

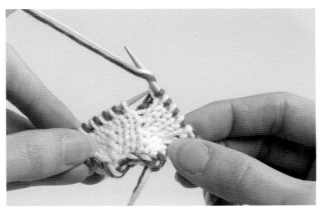

On the next row, knit the strand of the main color through the back loop with its matching yarn...

...and purl the strand of contrasting color through the back loop with its matching yarn.

Decreasing

Left-slanting Decrease

*
Slip the first (knit) stitch of the stitch pair purlwise with both yarns in back.

Slip the next 2 stitches (the purl from the 1st stitch pair and the knit from the following stitch pair) knitwise. Slide the 2 stitches just slipped knitwise back onto the left needle. The stitches have changed places and there are now 2 knits followed by 2 purls.
*

Insert the left needle into the back of the two twisted stitches on the right needle and slip them back onto the left needle.

Knit the next knit stitch through the back, then pass the original slipped stitch over.

Move both yarns to the front and slip the next stitch purlwise...

...purl the next stitch...

...and pass the slipped stitch over.

Right-slanting Decrease

Work the first 3 steps, from * to *, as for the left-slanting decrease.

Slide the original slipped stitch back onto the left needle.

Knit 2 together with the main color.

Purl 2 together with the contrasting color.

Short Row Turns

To avoid creating holes when turning in the middle of the row on short rows, work special turning stitches:

After turning, slip the first stitch purlwise with yarn in front.

Pull the working yarn to the back over the top of the needle. The stitch now has both legs on the needle.

Work the turning stitch the same way on the knit and purl of each stitch pair, slipping 1 stitch purl wise, then pulling the yarn over the top of the needle to the back so both legs of the stitch are around the needle.

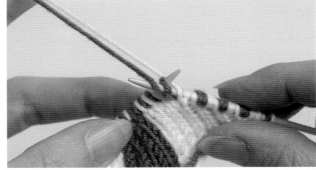

On the next row, work both legs of the turning stitch together as one stitch, whether it is a knit or a purl.

One-color Bind-Off

*Slip the second stitch (purl) of the stitch pair over the first stitch (knit), and drop it from the left needle. Then knit the knit stitch with the main color. Rep from *, then pass the second stitch on the right needle over the first.

Repeat until all stitches have been bound off. Cut both yarns and pull the tails through the last loop to fasten off.

Binding Off

Two-color Bind-Off

Working with both strands of yarn held together, knit both parts of the next stitch pair together as one stitch, knit the next stitch pair in the same manner, then pass the second stitch from the tip of the right needle over the first.

Repeat until all stitches have been bound off. Cut both yarns and pull the tails through the last loop to fasten off.

Yarn Information

Westminster Fibers (US)
8 Shelter Drive
Greer, SC 29650
info@westminsterfibers.com
www.westminsterfibers.com

Webs – America's Yarn Store
75 Service Center Road
Northampton, MA 01060
800-367-9327
www.yarn.com
customerservice@yarn.com

If you are unable to obtain any of the yarn used in this book, it can be replaced with a yarn of a similar weight and composition. Please note, however, the finished projects may vary slightly from those shown, depending on the yarn used.

For more information on selecting or substituting yarn contact your local yarn shop or an online store, they are familiar with all types of yarns and would be happy to help you. Additionally, the online knitting community at Ravelry.com has forums where you can post questions about specific yarns. Yarns come and go so quickly these days and there are so many beautiful yarns available.

About the Author

Anja Belle, née Goldstein, born in 1972, is a master photographer, married, and the mother of two sons.

After her sons were born, she hung up her camera and began to knit and explore her creativity. She lives with her family in Langenselbold, Germany and has worked as a knitwear designer for some time now. She has published many knitting designs and is active on Ravelry under her pseudonym, "Kalinumba."

Learn more on her website (www.kalinumba.com) and blog (www.kalinumba.wordpress.com).

For my two sons Paul and Max.

Abbreviations

beg	begin, beginning
BO	bind off (British cast off)
cm	centimeter(s)
CO	cast on
dec	decrease
dpn(s)	double-pointed needle(s)
g	gram(s)
gauge	British tension
in	inch(es)
inc	increase
k	knit
k2tog	knit two together
k3tog	knit three together

kf/b	knit into front and then back of same stitch
m	meter(s)
ndl(s)	needle(s)
p	purl
p2tog	purl two together
rep	repeat
rnd(s)	round(s)
St st	Stockinette stitch (British stocking st)
st(s)	stitch(es)
yd(s)	yard(s)
yo	yarnover

Acknowledgments

I would like to thank my family for their patience, Mrs. Uta Schurkart, Linda Hartenberger and Carmen Toledo-Holstein for their dedication, my parents for my knowledge and the creativity they have given me, the Hanauer Knitting Group for their curiosity and the relentless question, "When are you going to write a book?" and the many hardworking helpers behind the scenes who believed in me.